Where He Meets Me

Devotions from the Middle of Real Life

SAMANTHA MCCORMACK

Printed in the United States of America.

ISBN: 978-1-966723-38-7 (paperback)

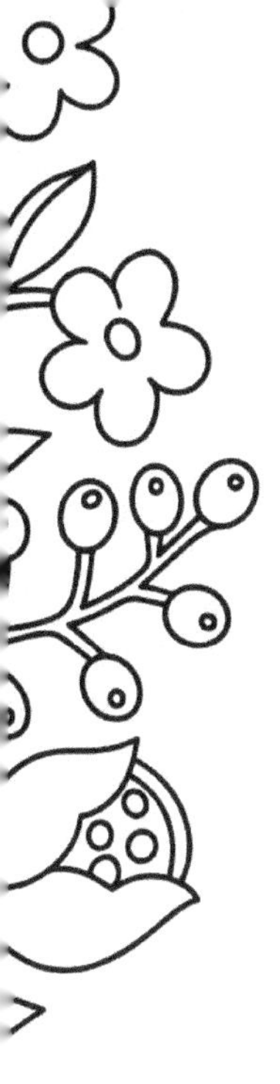

Dedication

To the ones with hands full and hearts wide open, who love Jesus deeply but often wonder if they are doing enough, this is for you.

To the woman who worships while folding laundry, prays between errands, and pours out her soul between the quiet and the chaos, you are not forgotten.

To the weary disciple in the thick of motherhood, marriage, work, ministry, or simply making it through, may these words meet you where you are.

To Sahra, my sweet girl, you inspire me daily to choose grace over perfection and presence over pressure. May you always know that God's love is not earned, it is embraced.

And to the Gentle Shepherd who walks beside us when we're strong, when we're stretched thin, and even when we are unsure, this offering is Yours.

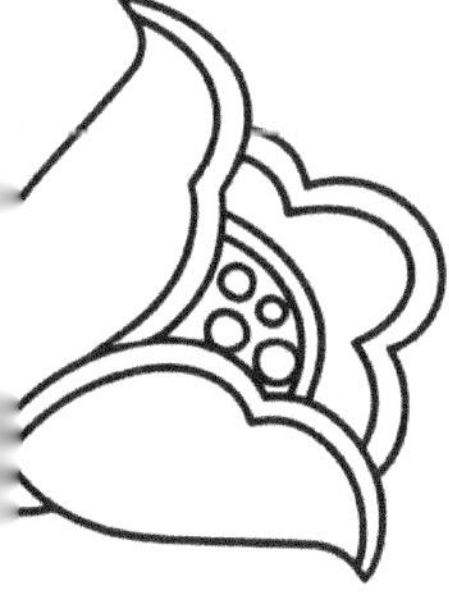

"...He gently leads those that have young." Isaiah 40:11 (NIV)

Acknowledgments

To every woman who shared her story, struggle, or strength with me, thank you. Your vulnerability gave voice to these pages.

To my husband, Patrick, thank you for holding space for me to write, dream, and rest. Your support makes room for my soul to breathe.

To my daughter, Sahra, your joy and curiosity reminded me to slow down and notice God's grace in the small, sacred things.

To my mom, for your love, faith, and unwavering support. Thank you for unknowingly teaching me how to pray and pen my thoughts out to Jesus.

To the sisters, friends, and encouragers who reminded me to keep going when I questioned my voice, I thank God for you.

To the Holy Spirit, who whispered when I was weary, inspired when I was empty, and stayed when I was stuck. Every word is because of You.

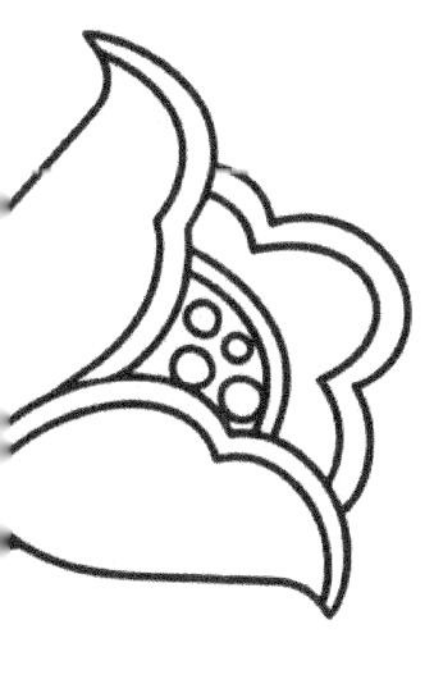

Table of Contents

Introduction

This devotional was born out of my own wrestling.

I love Jesus deeply, yet I have often found myself buried under the weight of expectations both spoken and silent. The lists. The roles. The pressure to do more, be more, give more.

I have worn many hats: nurse, wife, mother, daughter, friend, servant. Somewhere between potty training, late-night prayers, meal prepping, and work moments, I realized I was showing up *for* God, but not always *with* Him.

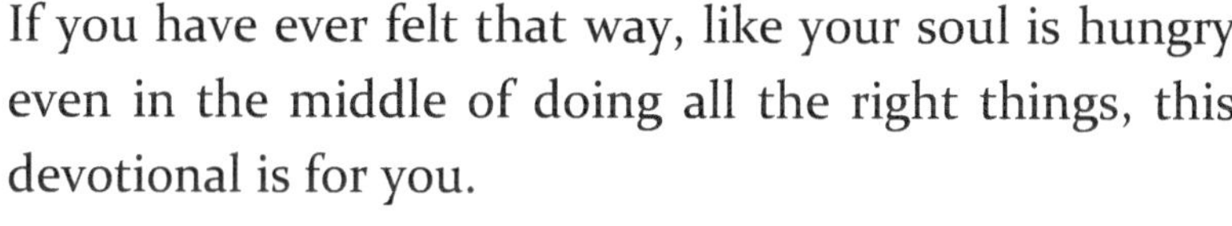

If you have ever felt that way, like your soul is hungry even in the middle of doing all the right things, this devotional is for you.

Here, I invite you to slow down. Breathe. Reflect. Listen.

These pages will not give you more to do. They will simply remind you of what is already true: God is with you, delighted in you, and inviting you to walk with Him, not in striving, but in stillness.

The Holy Spirit is a Gentleman who does not force His way in but waits to be invited. Invite Him into the chaos, and you will realize this is where He meets you the most.

Section 1

Entering In—Foundations of Worship and Connection (Days 1-7)

This first section is an invitation to step into God's presence with a tender heart and open hands. It centers you in worship (He inhabits our praises) and reminds you that before anything else, you are loved, welcomed, and invited to connect deeply with the One who delights in being with you.

Day 1

Enter His Gates with Thanksgiving

SCRIPTURE

"Enter His gates with thanksgiving: go into His courts with praise. Give thanks to Him and praise His name."— Psalm 100:4 (NLT)

DEVOTIONAL

Starting our day by entering God's presence with thanksgiving is a powerful act of faith and surrender. When we choose to come before Him with a grateful heart, we shift our focus from life's challenges to His goodness. The psalmist reminds us that thanksgiving is the key that unlocks the gates to His presence, while praise draws us deeper into His courts.

When we enter God's gates with thanksgiving, we acknowledge His blessings, big and small. It's an intentional act of looking at our circumstances and finding reasons to be grateful, even in seasons of hardship. Thanksgiving is not just a response to our blessings; it is a declaration of trust in God's faithfulness. As we thank Him, we affirm that He is at work in every detail of our lives.

The courts of praise signify a deeper intimacy with God. Praise goes beyond expressing gratitude for what He

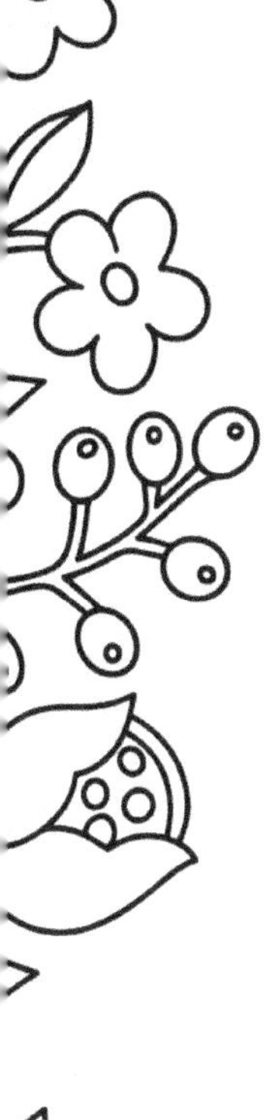

has done, it celebrates who He is. As we lift our voices in praise, we are inviting God's presence into our midst. I equate this posture of entering into worship to when you are just getting acquainted with a friend. You tend to keep them in the living room, where it is probably tidier than the rest of the house. Then, as you get closer and get to know each other better, you feel free to show them your bedroom, which at times can be messy. I consider this the inner courts; this is where God's presence is. The Bible tells us that God inhabits the praises of His people (see Psalm 22:3). This means He dwells and moves in the atmosphere of praise. When we praise Him, we create a space where He can work in our hearts, bringing transformation, healing, and peace.

REFLECTION

Begin today by listing three things you are thankful for.

Spend a few moments praising God for who He is: faithful, loving, and ever-present.

Think about how God's presence changes the atmosphere when you praise Him. How can you make praise a daily habit?

SONG SUGGESTIONS

"Give Thanks" by Don Moen, "So Good" by Elevation Worship and "Everything" by TobyMac

PRAYER

Lord, I come into Your presence with a heart full of gratitude. Thank You for Your goodness and faithfulness in my life. Help me to cultivate a lifestyle of thanksgiving, always finding reasons to praise You, regardless of my circumstances. As I praise You, may Your presence fill my life, bringing peace and joy that surpasses all understanding. Inhabit my praise, Lord, and let Your glory be revealed in every situation. In Jesus' name. Amen.

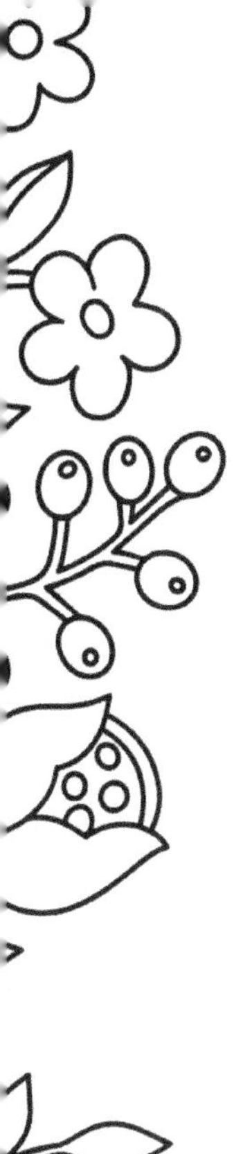

Day 2

Loving Jesus Above All

SCRIPTURE

"Whom have I in heaven but You? I desire You more than anything on earth." — Psalm 73:25 (NLT)

Spend a few minutes listening to "I Love You Jesus More Than Anything" by Maranda Curtis. Let the melody and lyrics guide your time of worship. As you listen, pour out your heart in thanksgiving and allow your love for Jesus to grow deeper.

DEVOTIONAL

There was a time in my life when praising God felt hard, and all I wanted to do was to whine and complain about how my life was nowhere near what I wanted, how much I was struggling, and like the Pharisees say, *"I tithe all the time. I fast. I am always present and willing to serve at church."* But that was getting me nowhere with God. I am reminded of what my praise and worship mean to God. You see, the Holy Spirit is a gentleman who does not force His way into our lives. He waits patiently for us to invite Him, showing us that true love comes through free will.

Praise becomes a doorway that invites the Holy Spirit into our hearts, and this song expresses a heartfelt desire to put Jesus at the center of our affection and

devotion. It reminds us that loving Him above all else is the greatest privilege and honor we can offer as believers. There are so many distractions that often pull at our heart's devotion. It could be worries about the future, the pursuit of material things, or even the demands of our daily responsibilities. Yet, in the quietness of our hearts, there is a place only Jesus can fill. The psalmist's cry in Psalm 73:25 is a declaration of surrender: *"Whom have I in heaven but You? I desire You more than anything on earth" (NLT).* It reflects a heart that finds its satisfaction in God's presence above all things.

Today, set aside the noise and busyness. Come before Him with praise and thanksgiving, letting the song be your expression of love. Tell Jesus how much you love Him, not for what He can do, but for who He is. Recount the ways He has shown His faithfulness and express your gratitude for His love that never fails. As you do, let the love you have for Him surpass any other attachment or desire.

PRAYER

"Lord, I love You more than anything. There is no one and nothing on this earth that compares to You. You are the One my soul longs for, and today, I place You at the center of my heart. I thank You for Your love, which has never wavered, and for Your grace, which has carried me through every season. I pray that my life continually reflects a deep love for You above all else. In Jesus' name. Amen."

REFLECTION

Write down three things that you are grateful for today.

Consider how you can make time each day to express your love to Jesus, starting with a moment of praise.

Day 3

The Power of God's Presence

SCRIPTURE READING

Then Moses said, "If you don't personally go with us, don't make us leave this place. How will anyone know that you look favorably on me and on your people if you don't go with us? For your presence among us sets your people and me apart from all other people on the earth." Exodus 33:15-16 (NLT)

REFLECTION

In Exodus 33, Moses leads the Israelites through the wilderness. The journey is daunting, filled with unknowns, barrenness, discomfort, and a sense of being alone. But Moses knows one truth that strengthens him: without God's presence, they cannot move forward. He does not just want God's blessings, protection, or even miracles; he yearns for God Himself. Moses realizes that God's presence alone will set them apart, sustain them, and bring true peace and fulfillment.

The same is true for us. We can go through life striving, planning, and hoping for things, but without God's presence, we will always feel empty, anxious, or lost. I know this is true for me when I go an extended period without my quiet times. There is this sense of busyness, but like I am getting nowhere, yet as soon as I get back

into God's presence, it brings me peace amid chaos, confidence in the face of fear, and joy that cannot be explained. Just as Moses desired to stay rooted in God's presence, so should we. We can tell God, *"If Your presence does not go with me, I do not want to go."* That is a declaration of total dependence on Him.

In Psalm 16:11, David beautifully says, *"You will show me the way of life, granting me the joy of your presence and the pleasures of living with You forever." (NLT).* This verse reminds us that fullness of joy, true peace, and a sense of purpose are found only in His presence.

Today, let your heart echo the prayer of Moses. Rather than seeking specific answers or blessings, simply rest in the beauty of being with God. Let His presence be your comfort, strength, and delight. Exalt your King for who He is. Let Him know how awesome He is, that there is none to be compared to Him. He is from everlasting to everlasting. He is worthy to be praised. He is not like other gods who have ears but cannot hear, eyes but cannot see; but He is all-seeing, all-powerful, all-knowing, and He is a God who does not grow weary. Just pour out your worship to Him. He longs to hear you exalt Him for who He is, not just for what He can do.

PRAYER

Father, I long for Your presence more than anything else. I know that without You, I cannot truly live. Let my heart be anchored in You, and may Your presence go with me wherever I go. Help me to remain close to

You, to listen to You, and to let Your peace fill my soul. You are my strength and portion. In Your presence, I am whole. In Jesus' name. Amen.

TIME OF WORSHIP

As you end this devotional time, enter a space of worship with God. Reflect on the songs below, letting the words remind you of the preciousness of God's presence:

— *"Your Presence is Heaven to Me" by Israel and New Breed*

As you sing this, let your heart meditate on the beauty of God's presence, realizing that there is nothing on earth that can satisfy like He does. His presence is a treasure, filling your soul with heavenly peace and joy.

— *"I Will Exalt You" by Todd Galberth*

This song is a declaration that God is the center of your life. As you sing, remind yourself that He is your God, and because of His presence, you have all you need. Worship Him as the one you exalt above all things.

— *"Great Are You Lord" by Todd Galberth*

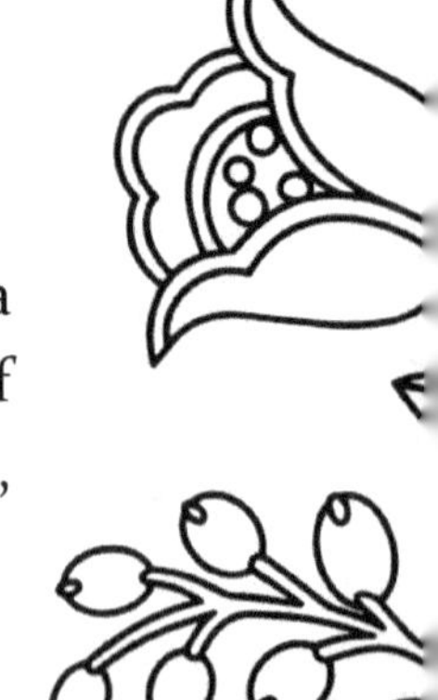

Let this song be a praise offering for who God is. It is a reminder of His greatness and power, and the joy of being in His presence. Pour out your praise as you sing, lifting up God for His majesty and love.

Today, rest in the assurance that His presence is with you. Just as Moses knew he could not move forward without God, make it your desire to seek His presence above all else. God is not only beside you but within you, guiding, comforting, and sustaining you. As you carry this truth into your day, remember that wherever you go, God's presence goes with you, and that is more than enough.

Day 4

Stay Alert and Guard Your Heart

SCRIPTURE

"But take heed to yourselves and be on your guard, lest your hearts be overburdened and depressed (weighed down) with the giddiness and headache and nausea of self-indulgence, drunkenness, and worldly worries and cares pertaining to [the business of] this life, and [lest] that day come upon you suddenly like a trap or a noose;"
—Luke 21:34 (AMPC)

REFLECTION

When we think of spiritual pitfalls, our minds often go to the "big sins": drunkenness, adultery, stealing, or lying. But what about the subtle, everyday burdens we carry? These distractions may seem less dangerous, yet they can weigh us down and lead us into spiritual complacency. Reading this scripture was like an "ouch" moment for me. The Holy Spirit convicted me of my worry about our finances and what more we could do to get ahead. Here in Luke 21:34, Jesus offers a stern yet loving warning: *stay vigilant and guard your heart.* The cares of this world, whether they are the pursuit of pleasure, material gain, or the anxiety of daily struggles, can weigh us down spiritually. These burdens have the power to cloud our focus, distract us from God's

purpose, and lead us into a trap of spiritual complacency.

Jesus understood that life's distractions could numb our spiritual senses. The "giddiness and headache" described here represent the fleeting highs and inevitable crashes of overindulgence, while "worldly worries" symbolize the endless cycle of anxiety about things we cannot control. These distractions keep us tethered to the temporary instead of the eternal.

PERSONAL APPLICATION

Think about what weighs you down today. Is it the pressure to achieve, the fear of tomorrow, or the temptation to indulge in what feels good but is not good for you? Jesus invites us to cast these cares on Him (see 1 Peter 5:7) and to keep our hearts fixed on Him.

To guard your heart means to remain spiritually awake and align your priorities with God's Word. It is about replacing the fleeting highs of this world with the lasting joy of His presence. Ask yourself: *What steps can I take today to remain alert and safeguard my heart?*

GRATITUDE

Write out three things you are grateful for today. It could be gratitude for having somewhere to sit and have quiet time with God today.

SONG FOR THE HEART

— *"Turn Your Eyes Upon Jesus" by Helen H. Lemmel.*

PRAYER

Lord, thank You for reminding me to guard my heart against the distractions and burdens of this life. Help me to fix my eyes on You and not be consumed by self-indulgence or worry. Give me discernment and strength to walk faithfully with You, trusting in Your provision and grace. Let me be ever watchful and ready for Your return. In Jesus' name. Amen.

CHALLENGE FOR TODAY

Spend 10 minutes reflecting on what areas of your life may be overburdened or distracted. Surrender them to God in prayer, and choose one practical way to stay spiritually alert this week.

Day 5

What Will God Do With This?

SCRIPTURE READING

Another of His disciples, Andrew, Simon Peter's brother, said to Him, There is a little boy here, who has [with him] five barley loaves, and two small fish; but what are they among so many people? John 6:8-9 (AMPC)

REFLECTION

The feeding of the 5,000 and the 4,000 are powerful reminders of God's ability to take what seems insufficient and make it more than enough. In John 6, Andrew questioned the smallness of the boy's lunch in light of the crowd's need. From a human perspective, the resources available seemed laughable. But what Andrew overlooked was the history they had with Jesus, the miracles, the provision, the unexplainable abundance.

Dr. Charles Stanley challenges us to take a different view. Instead of asking, *"What good is this?"* in difficult situations, ask, *"God, what are You going to do with this?"* It shifts our perspective from doubt to expectation. This message could not have come at a better time for my family and me, as I recall taking a nursing assignment in Missouri. We were driving through St. Louis when a hailstorm struck. Granted, I have never experienced a hailstorm in my life; we just heard things hitting the car. Sure, our windshield got damaged (we just got that car 3 days prior). I was like, "Really?" We had to get a new car due to engine problems, and now we had a cracked windshield. Through this process, we got our windshield fixed with no out-of-pocket cost and received an extra $300. What can God do with this?

Think about your own life. Maybe you feel like Andrew, looking at a situation that seems overwhelming: financial strain, a strained relationship, or an uncertain future. Perhaps you have seen God provide in the past, but now you are questioning, *"How far will this go?"*

When we bring our "not enough" to Jesus, He not only meets the need but exceeds it in ways we could never imagine. Faith is not about having all the answers; it is about trusting the One who does.

GRATITUDE MOMENT

Take a moment to reflect on a time when God provided for you in an unexpected way. Write it down and thank Him for it.

SONG FOR THE DAY

— *"Do It Again" by Elevation Worship*

A reminder that God is faithful to move again in your life, just as He has done before.

PRAYER

Lord, I bring my insufficiencies, doubts, and struggles before You today. I ask not, *"What good is this?"* but, *"What will You do with this?"* Help me to trust in Your provision and remember the miracles You have already performed in my life. Open my eyes to see the abundance You have already prepared. In Jesus' name. Amen.

REFLECTION QUESTION

What situation in your life feels overwhelming right now?

How can you surrender it to God with the expectation that He will use it for His glory?

Day 6

Be It Unto Me: A Heart of Submission

SCRIPTURE

Then Mary said, "Behold the maidservant of the Lord! Let it be to me according to your word." And the angel departed from her. Luke 1:38 (NKJV)

REFLECTION

What a Christmas story in the middle of the year! Yes, this one is a heart of submission to God. When Mary encountered the angel Gabriel, her initial reaction was one of confusion and questioning: *"How can this be, since I do not know a man?" (Luke 1:34 - NKJV).* She was faced with a life-altering revelation: a virgin carrying the Son of God! This was not an easy task, nor was it free from challenges. Imagine the potential ridicule, misunderstanding, possibility that her fiancé would not marry her, and even the danger she faced.

Yet, despite her questions, Mary chose faith over fear. Her ultimate response was not focused on her circumstances but on God's ability: *"Be it unto me according to your word."* Mary surrendered her plans, fears, and understanding to the Lord, trusting that His Word would accomplish what it said. What a reminder to me in a time of house hunting, and the Lord telling

us to pause. *Aww, what, Lord?* The market is a buyers' market, but nevertheless, be it according to Your Word.

Submission does not mean the absence of questions; it means trusting God beyond what we can see or comprehend. Just as Mary did, we may face seasons when God's plans seem impossible or too overwhelming. In those moments, we are invited to say, *"Lord, I do not understand it all, but I trust You."*

PERSONAL REFLECTION

What has God called you to do that feels overwhelming or uncertain?

Are you holding on to control, or are you willing to surrender and say, *"Let it be to me according to Your Word?"*

A GRATEFUL HEART

Today, write down three things you're grateful for in your current season. Gratitude often shifts our perspective from worry to trust.

A SONG FOR THE JOURNEY

— *"Trust in God" by Elevation Worship*

PRAYER

Lord, thank You for Your Word and Your promises. I may not always understand Your plans, but I choose to trust You. Like Mary, I submit my will to Yours, believing that You will bring to pass everything You have spoken over my life. Strengthen my heart to walk in faith, not fear. In Jesus' name. Amen.

CHALLENGE FOR THE DAY

Take one step of faith toward something God has placed on your heart. Trust that His Word will guide you, just as it did for Mary.

Day 7

When Faith Feels Like Falling

SCRIPTURE

The L*ORD directs the steps of the godly. He delights in every detail of their lives. Though they stumble, they will never fall, for the* L*ORD holds them by the hand. – Psalm 37:23-24 (NLT)*

REFLECTION

Walking in faith is not always as straightforward as we hope. Sometimes, we feel an unmistakable nudge from God to move in a certain direction, whether it is starting a new venture, relocating, or making a big life decision. We take the step, feeling confident in the Lord's guidance, but then challenges arise. Suddenly, we question everything. *"Did I really hear from God? Did I make a mistake?"* These are doubts and questions that plague our minds. Decisions do not come easily to me at times, as I feel a sense of fear: *What if I am moving against God's will? Is this the right time? Is this the right move?*

These moments can be discouraging. When things go wrong or take longer than expected, we tend to beat ourselves up, thinking we have failed or misunderstood God. But Psalm 37 reminds us that even when we fall, or when circumstances feel like a setback, we are never beyond God's hand. He doesn't leave us to figure it all

out alone. He orders our steps, delights in our journey, and upholds us when we stumble.

Walking in faith means trusting that God's plan is bigger than what we see. A fall does not mean failure; it is often part of the process. God uses even the hard moments to grow us, refine us, and remind us of our dependence on Him.

SONG FOR THE HEART

— *Oceans (Where Feet May Fail) by Hillsong United*

PERSONAL REFLECTION

Think back to a time when you stepped out in faith. What challenges arose? How did you respond? Did you see God working, even in the difficulty?

If you're in the middle of questioning your decisions or facing challenges today, remember that God is with you. He knew the obstacles you would face before you did, and He has already provided the strength you need to endure.

GRATITUDE

Write three things you are grateful for today. For example, *"I am grateful for the challenges I face when I step out in faith, as they have been lessons I have ended up sharing with others who are making similar steps of faith."*

ENCOURAGEMENT

When you feel the weight of doubt, go back to Psalm 37:23-24. Meditate on the truth that God delights in your steps, even when they are not perfect. Trust that He is holding you, and He will guide you through every challenge. You do not need to have it all figured out; you only need to keep trusting Him.

PRAYER

Father, thank You for ordering my steps. Sometimes, I feel uncertain and doubt the decisions I have made in faith. Forgive me for the times I have been hard on myself. Help me to trust that You are working, even when I face challenges. Thank You for upholding me when I stumble, and reminding me that Your plan is always greater than my fears. Teach me to walk in faith, leaning on Your strength and Your promises. In Jesus' name. Amen.

As you go through today, remember that your faith walk is not about perfection; it is about persistence. Trust that God's hand is always there to catch you.

Section 2

In the Tension—Emotions, Mind Battles, and Real Life (Days 8-14)

Life with God is beautiful, but it is also real. This section gives permission to acknowledge the internal battles we carry, the fear, anxiety, inadequacy, and weariness. Here, grace meets you in your honest moments and reminds you that God is not distant from your struggle; He is present in it and concerned about you.

Day 8

Grace for a Calm Heart

SCRIPTURE READING

Do not fret or have any anxiety about anything, but in every circumstance and in everything, by prayer and petition (definite requests), with thanksgiving, continue to make your wants known to God." – Philippians 4:6 (AMPC)

DEVOTIONAL

There are moments when the weight of anxiety feels unbearable, and the pounding of my heart seems to echo my inner chaos. These moments come when I want to rest from toiling all day, but my mind is racing how many miles per second, so rest seems hard to come by. It is in these moments that I am reminded of God's invitation to come to Him with my burdens. He does not promise to make life instantly easy (if I am being honest, life being easy is sometimes the cry of my heart), but He does promise His peace, a peace so profound that it defies explanation.

Anxiety and heart palpitations can be scary. They feel like a storm raging within, but God's Word reminds us that He is the calm in the storm. When the disciples feared the storm, Jesus spoke, *"Peace! Be still!" (Mark 4:39 - NKJV)*. That same voice speaks to my heart today. I am learning to lean into His Word, to pause and

breathe deeply, and to trust in the promise that He is guarding my heart and mind.

GRATITUDE

Write three things you are grateful for today. For me, I am grateful for the breath in my lungs today. I am grateful for the moments of peace, no matter how brief.

SONG FOR THE HEART

— *"It Is Well With My Soul" by Kristene DiMarco*

Let this song wash over you, reminding you of the calm assurance we have in Jesus.

PRAYER

Lord, You know the battles I face with anxiety and the physical toll it takes on my body. Thank You for being my refuge when fear rises. I bring my worries to You, trusting in Your ability to calm my anxious heart and steady my beating chest. Surround me with Your peace and remind me that You hold every moment of my life in Your hands. Help me to trust You more deeply. In Jesus' name. Amen.

CHALLENGE FOR TODAY

Whenever anxiety arises today, take a moment to pause, breathe deeply, and say, *"Lord, I trust You."* Repeat this as many times as needed and meditate on Philippians 4:6-7.

Day 9

Grace for the Balancing Act

SCRIPTURE

Roll your works upon the Lord [commit and trust them wholly to Him; He will cause your thoughts to become agreeable to His will, and] so shall your plans be established and succeed. – Proverbs 16:3 (AMPC)

DEVOTIONAL

As moms, we often feel caught between two worlds: the desire to nurture our families and the passion to contribute through our careers. As a nurse who works three 12-hour shifts and can feel so tired after a shift or three, my family desires quality time, and I feel like I do not have much to give. It is easy to feel overwhelmed, questioning if we are doing enough in either role. But God did not design us to carry the weight of perfection.

He sees your heart, efforts, and sacrifices. He knows the moments you have spent praying for wisdom on whether to step back or step forward. It is not about choosing one over the other; it is about trusting Him to guide you in this season.

Maybe today, you need to hear this: *You are enough.* Whether you are at home full-time, working part-time, or building a career, God can use your story to bless

your family and others. Trust Him to fill the gaps where you feel stretched thin.

When the thoughts of inadequacy bombard you, remember that your identity is not found in what you do but in who God says you are: *His beloved daughter, perfectly loved and equipped for the journey.*

GRATITUDE

Write three things you are grateful for. For me, I am grateful for the privilege of being a mom, and thankful for God's guidance as I navigate my roles.

SONG

— *"See the Goodness of the Lord" by VaShawn Mitchell (feat. Donnie McClurkin*

PRAYER

Father, thank You for seeing my heart and struggles. Teach me to rest in Your grace and trust You to guide my steps as a mom and in my career. Help me to let go of the need for perfection and to focus on Your calling for me in this season. Strengthen me to navigate the balancing act with faith and peace. In Jesus' name. Amen.

Day 10

My Anxious Thoughts

SCRIPTURE

In the multitude of my [anxious] thoughts within me, Your comforts cheer and delight my soul! - Psalm 94:19 (AMPC)

REFLECTION

Anxiety has a way of creeping into the corners of our minds, whispering lies about our circumstances, our future, and even our worth. There are times, as women, our minds have like 80 tabs open, and we feel like we are not getting a lot done, but Psalm 94:19 reminds us that even when anxiety feels overwhelming, God offers consolation that brings joy. This is not a fleeting happiness but a deep, abiding joy rooted in His presence and promises.

There have been times in my life when I felt paralyzed by uncertainty. I questioned my choices, abilities, and even my purpose. Yet, in those moments, when I brought my concerns to God, His Word spoke peace to my soul. A specific moment came to mind when I was overwhelmed by financial burdens. I was looking into investments because I had zero knowledge of them—basic things like maximizing my retirement account. Everything felt so daunting, like I was at ground zero, and just as I was about to put my phone down, the

scripture quoted above came to mind. I read this verse, and it felt as if God was reminding me to rest in Him. Slowly, I felt the heaviness lift as His promises of provision and care filled my heart with joy.

The Hebrew word for "consolation" implies comfort and encouragement. It shows that God does not just remove our fears; He replaces them with the reassurance of His love, guidance, and power. His comfort becomes the anchor that steadies us, even when life feels chaotic.

SONG ON MY HEART

— *"More Than Able" by Maverick City*

GRATITUDE

Write three things you are grateful for today.

I am going to challenge you to write down one area of your life that is causing anxiety. Spend 10 minutes in prayer, asking God to fill that space with His peace and joy. Then, search for a promise in scripture that addresses that fear and meditate on it throughout the day.

PRAYER

Lord, thank You for being my comforter when anxiety tries to overtake me. Help me to lay my burdens at Your feet, trusting that Your joy will replace my fear. Remind me daily of Your goodness, and let Your presence be my source of peace. In Jesus' name. Amen.

Day 11

Strength in Weakness

SCRIPTURE

But He said to me, My grace (My favor and loving-kindness and mercy) is enough for you [sufficient against any danger and enables you to bear the trouble manfully]; for My strength and power are made perfect (fulfilled and completed) and show themselves most effective in [your] weakness. Therefore, I will all the more gladly glory in my weaknesses and infirmities, that the strength and power of Christ (the Messiah) may rest (yes, may pitch a tent over and dwell) upon me! – 2 Corinthians 12:9 (AMPC)

DEVOTIONAL

Weakness is not failure; it is an invitation for God to step in. I remember a season during the infant stages when I had to go back to work. I was sleep-deprived and still had to work the long 12-hour shifts, and struggled to produce breast milk in the amount I wanted; finding it hard to have my devotions was enough for me to feel like I had failed somehow. It was a season when I felt completely drained emotionally, physically, and spiritually. I had nothing left to give. That's when I learned the power of surrender.

When you feel overwhelmed by doubt, remind yourself that God has equipped you with everything you need for the work He has called you to. You are not in this alone. He is your strength when you feel weak, your wisdom when you feel lost, and your courage when you feel afraid. Imposter syndrome loses its grip when we surrender our inadequacies to the One who is more than adequate. Take comfort in knowing that God chose you for this moment. He does not make mistakes, and His power is made perfect in your surrender.

Instead of trying harder or striving for more, I cried out to God, and He met me in my brokenness. His grace did not just sustain me; it transformed me. There is beauty in admitting, *"I can't do this alone."* When we allow God to take over, we experience His strength in ways we never imagined.

SONG

— *"Gracefully Broken" by Tasha Cobbs Leonard*

GRATITUDE

Write three things you are grateful for.

For me, I'm grateful for the moments when God's strength carries me, and I am blessed to know that even when I feel weak, He is my refuge.

PRAYER

Lord, thank You for Your grace that meets me in my weakness. Teach me to lean on You instead of my own strength. Remind me that Your power shines brightest when I surrender. Help me to see my struggles as opportunities to grow closer to You. In Jesus' name. Amen.

Day 12

Strengthened to Strengthen

SCRIPTURE

But I have prayed especially for you [Peter], that your [own] faith may not fail; and when you yourself have turned again, strengthen and establish your brethren. – Luke 22:32 (AMPC)

DEVOTIONAL

Sometimes, the battles we face come with a sense of shame. Maybe it is a financial mistake, sexual abuse, a broken relationship, or a sin we wrestled with for far too long. It can feel as though these experiences disqualify us or make us unworthy of God's love. But the truth is, whatever we go through, no matter how difficult or painful, is never wasted in God's hands.

Jesus knew Peter would deny Him, a moment that could have crushed Peter with guilt and shame. Yet, instead of letting Peter's failure define him, Jesus reassured him. He prayed that Peter's faith would not fail and declared that his turning back would lead to a powerful ministry of strengthening others.

In the same way, the situations that once brought us shame can become the very testimony that reminds others of God's unshakable love and faithfulness. It is not for us to lose heart or doubt His love; instead, it is an invitation to draw closer to Him. The trials, mistakes, and brokenness we face are often the tools God uses to build something new, something better, not just for us but for those who follow us.

Perhaps the cycle of shame ends with you, so your children never have to walk the same path. Maybe your testimony is the light someone else needs to find their way back to God. What the enemy meant for evil, God turns into a blessing.

SONG

— *"The Story I'll Tell" by Naomi Raine*

GRATITUDE

Write out three things you are grateful for.

For me, I am grateful that God does not call me by my mistakes or my shame but calls me His daughter.

PRAYER

Father, thank You for seeing beyond my failures, mistakes, and shame, and loving me still. Help me to trust in Your faithfulness, even when I feel unworthy. Please show me how to use my testimony to bring hope to others and to break cycles for the generations that follow me. Remind me that my story is a reflection of Your grace and not my shame. In Jesus' name. Amen.

ACTION STEP

Identify one situation in your life that brought shame or pain. Pray for God to heal your heart and show you how He can use it for His glory. Look for opportunities to encourage someone going through something similar this week.

Day 13

Declaring God's Favor in Every Season

SCRIPTURE

"For the Lord God is a Sun and Shield; the Lord bestows [present] grace and favor and [future] glory (honor, splendor, and heavenly bliss)! No good thing will He withhold from those who walk uprightly. – Psalm 84:11 (AMPC)

REFLECTION

Sometimes, we arrive where we feel called to be and yet struggle with feelings of doubt, insignificance, or a lack of favor. This feels true for me at times as a nurse. The days can be so long and hard that I doubt that I am where I need to be, and at times when I look around, it can seem like others are progressing or finding fulfillment in ways I am not. It is in these moments that God invites us to declare His favor, not based on what we see but on His promise.

God's Word reminds us that His favor is already on us. We do not have to earn it, and we do not need human validation to confirm it. Being where we are may not always feel fruitful or purposeful, but God assures us that nothing is wasted in His hands. He works, even in silence, even in seasons of hiddenness. Every moment can be a part of His process in shaping us and preparing

us for what's ahead. As Steven Furtick would say, *"What is now is connected to what is next."*

Think of Joseph in the Bible. God gave him visions of greatness, yet he found himself in pits, prisons, and places where favor seemed distant. But even in those challenging spaces, God's favor never left him. Through it all, God was preparing him, refining his character, and ultimately positioning him to save his family and countless others.

If you feel unseen or unappreciated where you are, remind yourself: *I am not overlooked by God.* Every detail of this season matters to Him. Let us choose to declare God's favor over our lives each day. Let's trust that He has us here for a reason, and in due time, He will reveal all things.

GRATEFULNESS

Write three things you are grateful for.

For me, I am grateful to the Lord for leading me to where I am today, even when the path feels uncertain.

SONG FOR MEDITATION

— *"Goodness of God" by CeCe Winans*

Let this song remind you of His constant goodness and faithful presence in every season.

DECLARATION OF FAITH

I declare God's favor over my life. I am not where I am by accident; God's hand is upon me.

I trust that where I am is part of His divine process. He is working in and through me, even in unseen ways.

I believe that God's favor opens doors no one can shut, and He will place me in positions that align with His will.

I am confident that the Lord has good plans for me, and I will flourish in His timing.

PRAYER

Lord, thank You for Your favor on my life. Even when I do not feel seen or valued, remind me that You have a purpose for me right where I am. Strengthen my faith to trust Your timing and to believe that every season holds value in Your kingdom. Help me to declare Your favor boldly and to walk with confidence, knowing that You are leading me. Let my life be a testimony of Your goodness and faithfulness. In Jesus' name. Amen.

Day 14

Victory Through Praise

SCRIPTURE

After consulting the people, the king appointed singers to walk ahead of the army, singing to the Lord and praising him for his holy splendor. This is what they sang: "Give thanks to the Lord; his faithful love endures forever!" — 2 Chronicles 20:21 (NLT)

DEVOTIONAL

Have you ever felt overwhelmed by a situation so daunting that you were not sure where to start? Maybe it is a health diagnosis, financial strain, relationship struggles, or the uncertainty of your future. These moments of feeling "surrounded" can leave us feeling afraid or powerless. Yet, the story of King Jehoshaphat in 2 Chronicles 20 shows us a different way to respond: through worship.

When King Jehoshaphat heard about the vast army approaching, he felt fear, just like any of us would. But his first response was not to strategize or prepare his forces. Instead, he called everyone to seek God together. Jehoshaphat prayed, acknowledging God's sovereignty, reminding himself and all of Judah of God's past faithfulness, and trusting that God would come through again.

What came next was unusual. Instead of soldiers, Jehoshaphat put singers at the front of his army. As they moved toward the battle, they praised God, singing, *"Give thanks to the Lord, for his love endures forever."* God responded by confusing the enemy forces, causing them to turn on each other, and Judah's army didn't even have to fight! Their victory came through faith, surrender, and worship.

In our own lives, praise can be a powerful act of faith. When we choose to praise God in the face of fear or uncertainty, we are essentially saying, *"God, I trust You. I believe You are greater than what I see before me."* Praise lifts our focus from our problems to God's power and goodness. It invites God to work in ways we may not expect.

SONG

— *"Surrounded (Fight my Battles)" by Michael W. Smith*

GRATITUDE

Write three things you are grateful for.

For me, I am grateful to have my quiet time today. This is sometimes hard with a toddler who is at the clingy stage, an early riser, and you are trying to enjoy every moment of it.

PRAYER

Lord, thank You for Your enduring love and faithfulness. Please help me to remember that the battles I face are not mine but Yours. Teach me to respond to challenges with worship and trust in Your power. As I praise You, I ask that You work in my situation in ways I can't even imagine. Give me faith to see victory through praise. In Jesus' name. Amen.

Section 3

God at Work—Trusting the Process (Days 15-21)

This section brings hope for the in-between seasons, when prayers linger unanswered, and detours seem endless. It reminds you that God is always at work behind the scenes, shaping the story, even when you cannot see the ending. His delays are not denials, and His timing is never wrong.

Day 15

From Ripened/Rotten Bananas to Divine Purpose

SCRIPTURE

And we know that God causes everything to work together for the good of those who love God and are called according to his purpose for them. — Romans 8:28 (NLT)

DEVOTIONAL

If you know me, you know the scripture above is one that I live by. Call it my anthem if you will. I have shared this scripture and the perspective I have gotten from it all the time. This was even engraved on the little notebooks we used for our wedding souvenirs.

Life can often feel like an unpredictable mix of ingredients, joys, sorrows, triumphs, and trials. Imagine these moments as individual ingredients in a recipe. Some ingredients, like sugar or flour, seem fine on their own, while others, like salt or baking powder, might taste bitter or unappealing alone. When mixed, however, these ingredients create something far more delicious and fulfilling than any one component could offer by itself.

Romans 8:28 reminds us that God sees every piece of our lives as part of a divine recipe. Just like an overly

ripe, rotten banana you might be tempted to toss, certain seasons in life feel too far gone or unpleasant to be useful. Yet, when God combines those "ripe banana" moments with other experiences, they transform into something good, like a nice banana bread.

God is the ultimate baker. In His hands, even what feels bitter, broken, or unappetizing becomes part of a greater, sweeter purpose. Every ingredient, every experience, is necessary to create the outcome He envisions. Our job is to trust Him in the process, even when it feels messy.

Whatever ingredient life throws your way today, remember that God is working it into His divine recipe. Trust that the final product will be good because it's in His hands.

SONG

— *"Intentional" by Travis Greene*

GRATITUDE

Write three things you are grateful for.

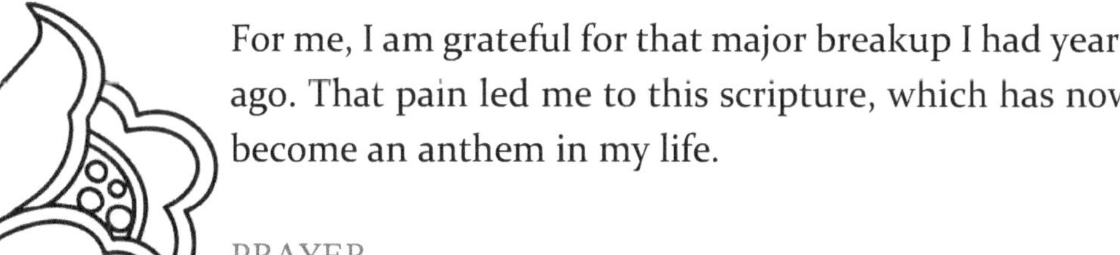

For me, I am grateful for that major breakup I had years ago. That pain led me to this scripture, which has now become an anthem in my life.

PRAYER

Heavenly Father, thank You for taking every part of my life, the good, the bad, and the seemingly unusable, and

working it together for Your glory and my good. Teach me to trust You with the difficult pieces, knowing that You see the final masterpiece. Help me to release my fears and doubts into Your hands, confident in Your wisdom. In Jesus' name. Amen.

Day 16

God Sees You in the Hard Places

SCRIPTURE

So she called the name of the Lord Who spoke to her, You are a God of seeing, for she said, Have I [not] even here [in the wilderness] looked upon Him Who sees me [and lived]? Or have I here also seen [the future purposes or designs of] Him Who sees me? – Genesis 16:13 (AMPC)

DEVOTIONAL

Hagar's story is one of pain, rejection, and ultimately redemption. She did not choose to be Sarai's maidservant or to be caught in the middle of Sarai and Abram's impatience with God's promises. Yet, she found herself in a hard place, cast out into the wilderness, feeling unseen and unloved.

But the God of all creation saw her. In her distress, He met her at the spring in the wilderness and made a promise to her and her son. Through no fault of her own, Hagar was placed in a situation that felt impossible. Yet, God turned her pain into purpose and her despair into hope.

Sometimes we find ourselves in hard spaces, situations that are not our fault but feel like a wilderness experience. The enemy whispers lies that we are alone, forgotten, or even that we deserve this suffering. I sure did feel this way through my painful breakup. I felt, somehow, it was my fault, but little did I know it was the will of God at that time, and just like Beyonce's song *"Thank God, I dodged a bullet,"* it became a phrase theme. Just as God saw Hagar, He sees you. His love does not waver when life is hard, and His provision is steadfast.

God is not just a God of the mountaintops; He is the God who meets us in the valleys and provides streams in the desert. Like Hagar, you may not have all the answers yet, but know this: God sees you, cares for you, and will provide in ways you cannot imagine.

SONG

— *"Isaiah Song" by Maverick City Music (Featuring Chandler Moore)*

GRATITUDE

Write three things you are grateful for.

For me, I am grateful for my now family. I did not dream it was possible, but God has been faithful, and He has heard and felt every tear and prayer.

PRAYER

Father, thank You for being the God who sees me. When I find myself in hard places, help me to remember that You are with me and Your provision is perfect. Teach me to trust You, even when I don't see the way forward. Just as You cared for Hagar and

Ishmael, I trust that You will care for me. In Jesus' name. Amen.

CHALLENGE FOR THE DAY

Take a moment to reflect on a hard place you have been through in your life. Write down how God provided for you during that time. Let it serve as a reminder of His faithfulness, even in the wilderness.

Day 17

Grace to Move Every Mountain

SCRIPTURE

Then he said to me, 'This is what the Lord says to Zerubbabel: It is not by force nor by strength, but by my Spirit,' says the Lord of Heaven's Armies. 'Nothing, not even a mighty mountain, will stand in Zerubbabel's way; it will become a level plain before him! And when Zerubbabel sets the final stone of the Temple in place, the people will shout: 'May God bless it! May God bless it!' – Zechariah 4:6-7 (NLT)

DEVOTIONAL

This text encourages us that God's Spirit, not our own strength, will overcome the mountains we face. Zerubbabel was tasked with rebuilding the temple; a job that seemed impossible in the face of obstacles. But God assured him that nothing, not even a mountain, would stand in his way; by God's Spirit, everything would be leveled.

This speaks deeply to my own life, especially as I think back to a time when I felt that my dreams were shut down. I had applied for a student visa to go to the United States, and after preparing, praying, and believing, I was denied. Not just once, but twice, including a denial for a visiting visa. I remember feeling bitterly disappointed, asking God why I was rejected,

and wondering if I had done something wrong. The most challenging part was watching the family I lived with at the time all receive their visas. They went on vacation that year, leaving me alone with a painful sense of being left behind, almost like God had forgotten or mocked me.

Looking back, I can now see how God was moving in a way I could not yet understand. Though I did not get my visa then, He was leveling mountains in His timing. Now, years later, I am in the very place I longed to be: not with just a visiting Visa but with a green card that afforded me to work and play like an American, not by my strength, but by His Spirit. That experience reminds me, even today, to trust that God is at work in every "no" and every closed door.

On your current journey, you may face some mountains: financial hurdles, career uncertainties, the walk of singleness, the challenges of parenting, and the need for healing in your marriage. But be encouraged that the same God who eventually brought you here is still moving mountains on your behalf. You can let go of striving in your strength, knowing that His Spirit is with you and will carry you through.

SONG

— *"For Every Mountain" by Kurt Carr and Kurt Carr Singers*

GRATITUDE

Write down three things you are grateful for.

For me, I am grateful that God's timing is perfect and that I was able to go to the US, especially during COVID, where I was able to work and even go to school.

PRAYER

Lord, thank You for reminding me that it's by Your Spirit, not my own strength, that I will overcome. I surrender my efforts and ask You to strengthen me where I feel weak. Father, level the mountains in my life and help me to trust Your perfect timing. Guide me, empower me, and give me the grace to move forward boldly in faith. In Jesus' name. Amen.

Day 18

Trusting God's Timing with Patience and Selflessness

SCRIPTURE

"Wait for the Lord; be strong, and let your heart take courage; wait for the Lord!" — Psalm 27:14 (ESV)

DEVOTIONAL

It's natural to feel frustrated when we are praying and waiting for God's answer, especially when it is about something pressing like a job or home ownership. Sometimes we can become so focused on our own needs that we overlook the bigger picture, God's bigger plan. Dr. Charles Stanley shared a profound insight on this. He reminded us that, in praying for a job, it is easy to want things immediately. Yet, God might be working in the lives of others too, shifting circumstances, touching hearts, and guiding others toward where they need to be before He opens the door for us.

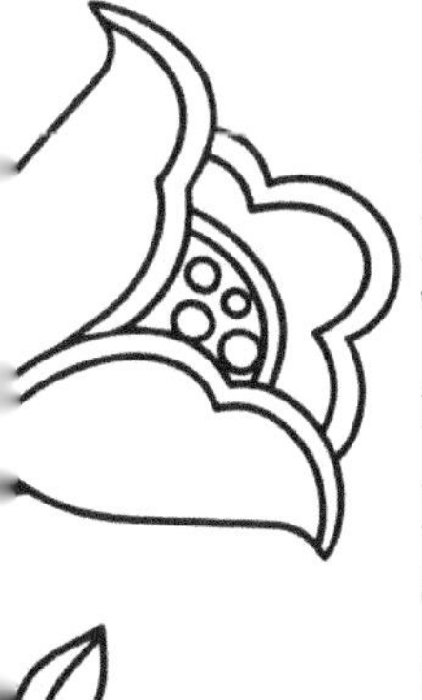

For example, imagine you are praying for a specific position, but someone else is currently in that role. They might be seeking a career change or needing time to recognize a new direction for their life. God, in His perfect timing, is working on both ends, preparing you and the person currently in the role. This process requires patience, not just because we are waiting on

God but because He is carefully orchestrating events for the good of everyone involved. This truth became very profound to me when I graduated from the University in Jamaica, and I was unable to get a job. During this season, I was babysitting my godson, which brought me so much joy, but I doubt it would have if God had not revealed this perspective on waiting for prayers to be answered. I answered a family's prayer while I waited for God to answer my need for a job.

This perspective reminds me of the importance of a selfless heart in prayer. Are we willing to wait patiently and trust God, knowing our prayer may involve more than just us? Can we release our desires to Him, confident that He is arranging things for the best, not just for us, but for others too? Patience in prayer is challenging, but when we understand that God's plans are complex and interwoven with others' lives, it becomes an opportunity to grow in faith and selflessness.

SONG

— *"See the Goodness" by VaShawn Mitchell (Feat. Donnie McClurkin*

GRATITUDE

Write three things you are grateful for. For me, I am grateful for the peace God gives me during times of waiting.

PRAYER

Heavenly Father, thank You for Your wisdom and perfect timing. Help me to wait with a patient heart, knowing You are at work in ways I cannot see. Teach me to be selfless in my prayers, remembering that Your plans reach far beyond my own needs. I trust You to open doors at the right time and to guide everyone involved in ways that bring You glory. In Jesus' name. Amen.

Day 19

It Had to Happen

SCRIPTURE

Jesus replied, 'You do not realize now what I am doing, but later you will understand.' — John 13:7 (NIV)

DEVOTIONAL

I never thought I would be fired. Not me. Not like that. I had worked hard, stayed committed, and tried to honor God, even when things were not perfect. So when it happened, it did not just surprise me, it hurt. It felt unfair, and all I could think was, *"Lord, I'm not prepared for this."*

I was back home in Jamaica. I had no idea what I was going to do next. I didn't even tell my family right away. Not because I wanted to hide, but because I didn't know how to speak my shame. I did not have answers. I did not have a plan. And most days, I did not feel peace; I just felt the weight of uncertainty.

It did not feel good, and I had no idea what God was up to. But even in that quiet and confusing space, I kept hearing this whisper in my spirit: *"Leave gracefully."* So I did. No bitterness. No loud exits. Just quiet trust that somehow God still had me, even if I did not understand how.

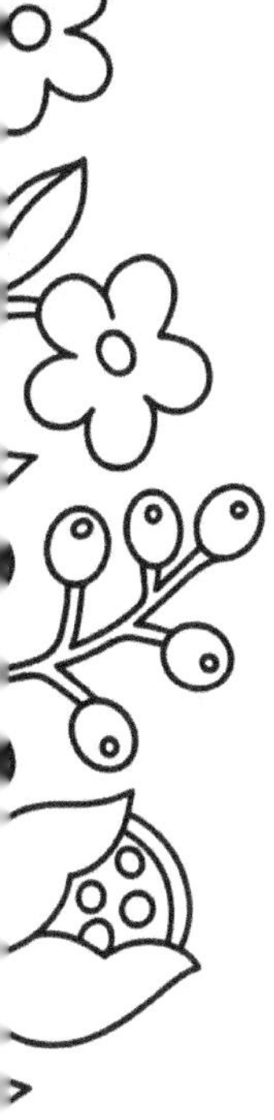

During that season, I came across a sermon by Steven Furtick called *"It Had to Happen."* I listened with tears in my eyes and a knot in my throat, because the message felt like it was written just for me.

Sometimes God closes doors that we do not feel ready to walk away from. Sometimes He allows the bottom to fall out, not to destroy us, but to deliver us. Sometimes, it really does *have* to happen so He can shift our direction. Tasha Cobbs says, *"When God breaks you, He does not destroy you."* He does it with grace.

What I did not know back then was that God was already making a way. That same year, I ended up teaching at a private school, a place that brought healing, purpose, and provision. And later, I migrated to the United States. One door closed, but so many others opened doors I never would have imagined if I had stayed where I was.

Jesus once told His disciples, *"You don't realize now what I am doing, but later you will understand."* And I have come to see He meant it. He still means it.

Even when life feels unfair—even when you are caught off guard—God is still working. And one day, it will all make sense.

SONG

— *"Refiner" by Maverick City Music (Feat. Steffany Gretzinger and Chandler Moore*

GRATITUDE

Write three things you are grateful for. Today, I am grateful that my daughter has two awesome grandmothers she gets to enjoy and be spoiled by.

PRAYER

Father, thank You for being faithful, even in the moments I didn't understand. When I felt unprepared, ashamed, and unsure, You were still at work. Thank You for every closed door that became a doorway into greater blessing. Teach me to trust You, not just when it makes sense, but even when it does not. I know now it had to happen. And You never waste a single step. In Jesus' name. Amen.

Day 20

When Life Does Not Go As Planned

SCRIPTURE

I returned and saw under the sun that the race is not to the swift nor the battle to the strong, neither is bread to the wise nor riches to men of intelligence and understanding nor favor to men of skill, but time and chance happen to them all. - Ecclesiastes 9:11 (AMPC).

Life often feels unpredictable, doesn't it? We work hard, plan carefully, and hope for the best, but sometimes the results do not match our efforts. This passage in Ecclesiastes reminds us that our abilities or wisdom do not always determine life's outcomes. Instead, there is an element of timing and divine orchestration beyond our control.

I was reminded of this truth during one of the most vulnerable moments of my life: the birth of my daughter. Everything was progressing well for a vaginal delivery, and I had reached 9 centimeters dilated. But as time passed, my baby wouldn't come, and her heart rate began to drop. What followed was an emergency C-section. I remember lying there, tears streaming down my face, feeling like I had failed. I had planned, prepared, and done everything right, but the outcome was not what I had envisioned (not remembering that I

did pray that we both would be healthy and safe during delivery, whether it was a vaginal or C-section delivery).

For weeks, I wrestled with feelings of inadequacy and disappointment. It was not until I brought my pain to God that I began to find peace. He gently reminded me that the value of my birth story was not in the method but in the miracle of life itself. God had brought my daughter into the world in His way and His timing, and that was something to celebrate, not mourn.

This can be frustrating if we rely solely on our strength or understanding, but it can also be a great comfort. We do not have to have all the answers because God does. We may not always understand why certain things happen, but we can trust that God's timing is perfect and His plans are good.

When life feels chaotic or unfair, lean on this truth: your worth is not determined by your success, and your failures do not define you. The most important thing you can do is trust in God's sovereignty and seek His guidance daily. He sees the whole picture of your life and knows exactly what you need and when you need it.

Today, let go of the pressure to have everything figured out. Instead, take a moment to pray and surrender your plans to God. Trust Him to guide you, even when life feels uncertain. Remember, He is faithful to place you in the right place at the right time for His glory and your good.

SONG

— *"In Control" by Hillsong*

GRATITUDE

Write three things you are grateful for. For me, I am grateful that my daughter gets to have her great grandma around, and to hear her say the words "great grandma."

PRAYER

Dear Heavenly Father, thank You for being in control, even when life feels uncertain. Help me to trust Your timing and plan, knowing that You see the full picture when I cannot. Teach me to rest in Your promises and find peace in Your sovereignty. Thank You for reminding me that my worth isn't determined by what I perceive as success or failure. In Jesus' name. Amen.

Day 21

Trusting God's Timing in the Waiting

SCRIPTURE READING

"So shall My word be that goes forth from My mouth; it shall not return to Me void, but it shall accomplish what I please, and it shall prosper in the thing for which I sent it." – Isaiah 55:11 (NKJV)

DEVOTIONAL

I remember a pivotal moment when my mom and I went to the embassy as part of our green card process. After the interview, we were left in uncertainty; they held on to my passport but did not tell us whether we had been approved. My mom was asked to submit an additional document, but her passport, her only form of ID, was what she had to use to get the document. It felt like we were stuck, unsure of what would happen next.

In the midst of that uncertainty, God spoke through my Bishop, reminding me of a powerful truth: *"Delay doesn't mean denial."* Those words became an anchor for my faith during that waiting period. They reminded me that even when we do not see immediate answers, God is still working behind the scenes to fulfill His promises.

Isaiah 55:11 tells us that God's Word will not return void. If He has spoken something over your life, you can trust that it will come to pass. The waiting period is not wasted time; it is a season where God strengthens our trust, deepens our faith, and shows us that His timing is perfect.

Philippians 4:19 reassures us that God will supply all our needs. Even as we waited for answers from the embassy, God provided for our daily needs and gave us the grace to keep moving forward. Looking back, I see that the delay was not a denial; it was part of God's plan to refine our faith and prepare us for what was to come.

SONG

— *"While I'm Waiting" by Travis Greene*

This song perfectly captures this faith-filled posture. It encourages us to trust God in the waiting, worship Him in the uncertainty, and hold onto the truth that His promises never fail.

GRATITUDE

Write three things you are grateful for.

PRAYER

Heavenly Father, thank You for reminding me that delay does not mean denial. Help me trust in Your timing and rest in the truth that Your Word will accomplish what You have spoken. I give You the areas of my life where I feel stuck or uncertain, knowing that

You are working all things together for my good. Thank You for supplying all my needs and for strengthening my faith in the waiting. In Jesus' name. Amen.

Section 4

Anchored Identity—Who God Says You Are (Days 22–25)

Sometimes we need to pause and ask, *"Who am I listening to?"* These devotions are gentle reminders to root your identity, not in performance, opinions, or comparison, but in God's unchanging truth. Peace flows from knowing who you are and whose you are.

Day 22

Your Chapter 2, Not Their Chapter 20 - The Pace of Purpose

SCRIPTURE

"This vision is for a future time. It describes the end, and it will be fulfilled. If it seems slow in coming, wait patiently, for it will surely take place. It will not be delayed." - Habakkuk 2:3 (NLT)

DEVOTIONAL

Have you ever scrolled through social media or listened to someone's story of success and thought, *I should be further along by now?* I have been there, especially after starting over when I moved to America. Everything felt like a reset. I saw friends buying homes, advancing in careers, or achieving goals that seemed so far out of reach for me.

I remember one night sitting with my journal and pouring my heart out to God. I was exhausted from comparing my beginning to someone else's highlight reel. It felt unfair, like I was stuck at Chapter 2 of my life while others were living in Chapter 20. I questioned whether I had made the right choices or if I would ever "catch up."

That is when the verse above from Habakkuk began to minister to me. It reminded me that purpose unfolds in

God's timing, not according to comparison or pressure. Even when progress feels slow, God is still at work. Delay does not mean denial, and waiting does not mean nothing is happening. What God has spoken over your life will come to pass, not a moment too early and not a moment too late.

Just as no one picks up a book and skips to Chapter 20 expecting to understand the story, we cannot rush ahead in our own lives. God is still writing our chapters, and each one has a purpose. Starting over was not a setback; it was part of the process, or, as my cousin would say, a way to get a fresh start.

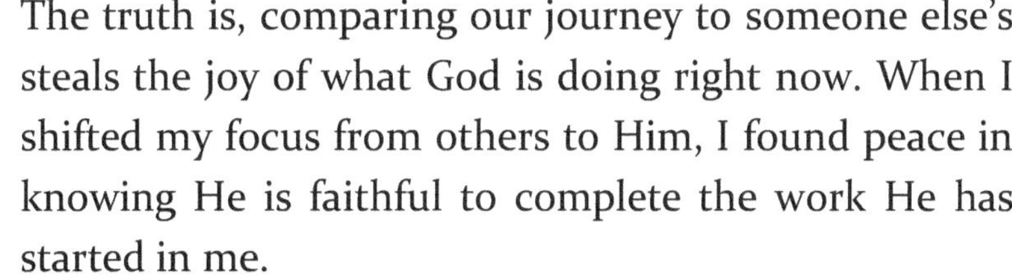

The truth is, comparing our journey to someone else's steals the joy of what God is doing right now. When I shifted my focus from others to Him, I found peace in knowing He is faithful to complete the work He has started in me.

SONG

— *"Wait on You" by Elevation Worship and Maverick City Music*

GRATITUDE

Write three things you are grateful for.

PRAYER

Lord, help me to focus on my own journey and trust the process You have set for me. Remind me that Your plans are perfect, and Your timing is always right.

When I am tempted to compare, show me how far You have brought me, and give me peace in this chapter of my life. In Jesus' name. Amen.

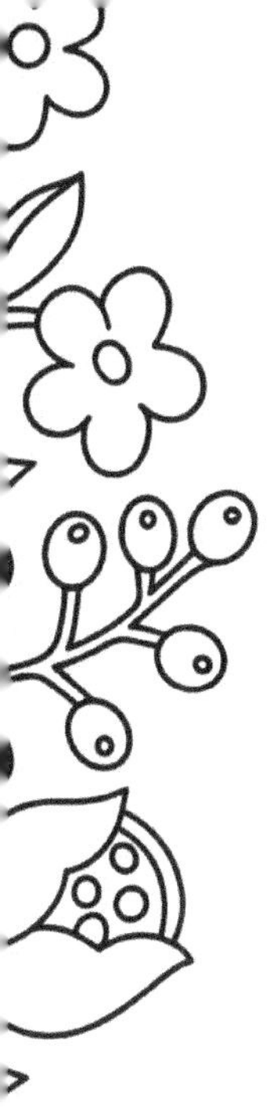

Day 23

Rearview Mirror

SCRIPTURE

Do not [earnestly] remember the former things; neither consider the things of old. Behold, I am doing a new thing! Now it springs forth; do you not perceive and know it and will you not give heed to it? I will even make a way in the wilderness and rivers in the desert. - Isaiah 43:18-19 (AMPC)

DEVOTIONAL

Have you ever found yourself constantly glancing at the rearview mirror while driving, even when it was not necessary? I often catch myself doing this, checking who's behind me, maybe speeding up if someone seems to be tailgating, or switching lanes to let someone pass. Recently, as I kept looking back, I felt the Holy Spirit ask, *"Why do you keep looking behind?"* And I heard this gentle reminder: *The reason the windshield is so much larger than the rearview mirror is because we are meant to focus more on what's ahead than on what's behind.*

Think about that. How often do we dwell on the past, replaying mistakes, regrets, past hurts, or even cherished memories, rather than keeping our eyes on what God is doing now? Isaiah 43:18-19 speaks directly to this struggle: *"Do not [earnestly] remember the former things; neither consider the things of old. Behold, I am doing a new thing! Now it springs forth; do you not perceive and know it and will you not give heed to it?"*

When we focus too much on the past, we risk missing the new work God is doing in our lives. Just as driving forward requires us to look through the windshield rather than fixate on the rearview mirror, our journey with God requires us to look ahead, trusting Him with what is ahead rather than what is already behind.

What are the "former things" you've been carrying with you? Is it a past hurt that is hard to let go of? Or maybe a time when you saw God's hand powerfully at work, and you wonder if He will ever move in the same way again? God assures us that He is doing something new, even now, and that He will make a way in the wilderness and bring rivers to desert places, promising life, hope, and His continual presence, even in the most barren seasons.

GRATITUDE

Write three things you are grateful for. For me, I am grateful for the gift of goodbye and that I am finding it easy to let things go.

SONG

— *"Moving Forward" by Israel Haughton*

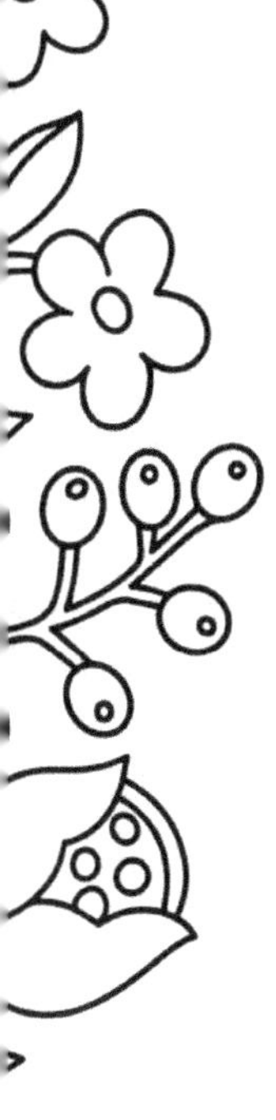

MOVING FORWARD IN FAITH

Letting go of the past is not easy, especially if it is something that impacted us deeply. But just as you only use the rearview mirror for brief glances to navigate an obstacle or make a quick adjustment, our past should serve only as a quick reference, not our main focus. We cannot move forward if we are continually acting on the impulses of what used to be. The broader view God has for us is up ahead, and His blessings add richness without sorrow (see Proverbs 10:22).

PRAYER

Heavenly Father, thank You for being my guide and refuge. I come before You today, surrendering my past into Your hands. I acknowledge that letting go is not always easy, but I trust that Your plans for me are far greater than anything behind me. I believe that the future You have for me is filled with purpose, hope, and joy. Open my eyes to see the new things You are doing in my life. Strengthen my faith to step forward boldly, knowing that You walk beside me. In Jesus' name. Amen.

Day 24

Whose Report Will You Believe?

SCRIPTURE

"Who has believed our report? And to whom has the arm of the Lord been revealed?" - Isaiah 53:1 (NKJV)

DEVOTIONAL

When facing a situation like an unexpected doctor's report, fear and doubt can creep in. Whether it's a diagnosis, complications in pregnancy, or other health concerns, these moments can challenge your faith. Sometimes it is even our body's symptoms, but no test results can tell you what is going on. But as children of God, we have a choice: *to focus on what man says or what God says.*

Imagine a mother who receives a report from her doctor about complications in her pregnancy. The doctor might say, *"We see internal bleeding, and there's a risk of miscarriage."* In that moment, she has a choice: either let fear dictate her response or stand on the Word of God. She begins to pray, *"Lord, You are the giver of life. I declare that this baby will live and not die. You have knit this child together in my womb, and I trust You to carry us both safely through this."* Months later, that same woman holds her healthy baby in her arms, a testimony to God's faithfulness.

In the Bible, we see countless examples of God's power overriding human understanding. Consider Sarah, who was barren yet gave birth to Isaac, or Hannah, who prayed fervently and received the child she longed for. Our God specializes in turning impossible situations into testimonies of His glory.

The enemy seeks to plant seeds of fear, but God reminds us that His report reigns supreme. God's report declares life, healing, and restoration. Doctors may have expertise, but their word is not the final word, God's is. The Creator of life is intimately involved in every detail, including the unseen battles in your body.

If you are walking through a season of uncertainty due to a medical report, declare God's promises over your situation. Speak life into your body and your circumstance:

- *"By His stripes, I am healed." Isaiah 53:5 (KJV).*
- *"He will give His angels charge over you, to keep you in all your ways." Psalm 91:11(KJV).*
- *"You formed my inward parts; You covered me in my mother's womb." Psalm 139:13(KJV)*

Remind yourself that God's power is limitless. The same God who parted the Red Sea, healed the woman with the issue of blood, and raised Lazarus from the dead is fighting for you.

SONG

— *"God Is Not Against Me" by Elevation Worship (feat. Jonsal Barrientes and Tiffany Hudson)*

GRATITUDE

Write three things you are grateful for today. For me, I am grateful that I have our baby girl and that we are both healthy and doing well after delivery. God is so faithful.

PRAYER

Heavenly Father, we thank You for being the God whose Word stands above all else. When we hear reports that cause fear or doubt, remind us of Your promises. Help us to trust You in the face of uncertainty. For anyone receiving difficult news about their health or pregnancy, we pray for Your peace that surpasses understanding. We declare life, healing, and restoration. Let Your glory be revealed in their story. In Jesus' name. Amen.

Day 25

Perfect Peace in Chaos

SCRIPTURE

"You will keep him in perfect peace, whose mind is stayed on You, because he trusts in You. Trust in the Lord forever, for in Yah, the Lord, is everlasting strength." — *Isaiah 26:3-4 (NKJV)*

DEVOTIONAL

There's a kind of peace that does not make sense, the kind where people look at your life and wonder why you are not falling apart. When the bills are piling up, when your marriage feels strained, when your dreams seem like they are on hold, by all accounts, you should be frantic. But you are not.

I remember sitting in my car, heart racing, thinking about everything I could not control. The what-ifs were loud, the fear was real. But in that moment, I whispered, *"God, I trust You."* It was not some grand declaration. It was a simple surrender. And somehow, peace settled in, a peace I could not explain, a peace that did not erase the problem but anchored my soul in the middle of it.

Isaiah reminds us that this peace is not found in fixing our circumstances but in fixing our eyes on God. The more we trust, the more we are kept in peace. This peace is not fragile; it is built on an everlasting Rock: a foundation that does not shake when life does.

Maybe today, your heart feels unsteady. Maybe your mind is running in circles, trying to figure things out. Take a deep breath. Whisper, *"God, I trust You."* Fix your mind on Him. His peace will meet you there.

GRATITUDE

Write three things you are grateful for today. For me, I am grateful for my husband, who loves to cook. I remember praying and saying I wanted a chef for a husband because I did not like cooking. Whelp! He is not a chef, but he loves to cook.

SONGS

— *"Christ Is My Firm Foundation (He Won't)" by Maverick City (feat. Chandler Moore and Cody Carnes).*

— *"God I Look to You" by Tasha Leonard*

PRAYER

Father, in the chaos, keep my mind stayed on You. When I feel overwhelmed, remind me that You are my Rock, steady, unshaken, and always faithful. I surrender my worries and choose to trust You. Let Your perfect peace guard my heart and mind today. In Jesus' name. Amen.

Section 5

Rooted and Secure—Living from Approval, Not For It (Days 26-29)

These final entries invite you to rest in God's approval. No more performing. No more striving to be "enough." You are already chosen, seen, and deeply loved. In this sacred space of security, you are free to flourish.

Day 26

Planted and Flourishing

SCRIPTURE

"He shall be like a tree planted by the rivers of water, that brings forth its fruit in its season, whose leaf also shall not wither; and whatever he does shall prosper." – Psalm 1:3 (NKJV)

DEVOTIONAL

Life can often feel like a whirlwind of uncertainty, financial pressures, relationship struggles, career doubts, and spiritual dryness. But Psalm 1 reminds us that a person who delights in the Lord and meditates on His Word is like a tree planted by streams of water.

Notice that the tree is planted. This means it did not grow randomly there; it was intentionally placed near a life-giving source. Likewise, when we root ourselves in God's Word, we are nourished, sustained, and able to stand firm through life's storms.

The verse also speaks of bearing fruit in its season. Sometimes, we feel frustrated because we do not see immediate results in our efforts, whether in parenting, marriage, finances, or spiritual growth. But trees do not bear fruit every day; they do so in their season. If we

remain steadfast in God, He will bring fruitfulness at the right time.

The promise continues, *"whose leaf shall not wither."* Even in difficult seasons, when we abide in God, we remain spiritually alive. While challenges may come, we will not wither away because our source of strength is unshakable.

GRATITUDE

Write three things you are grateful for today. For me, I am grateful I have a job that is able to finance our day-to-day expenses. We are so blessed, and I think I sometimes take this for granted: I am never hungry by force, but by choice.

SONG

— *"Build My Life" by Pat Barrett*

PRAYER

Lord, plant me firmly in Your Word. Let my roots go deep into Your truth so that I can stand strong in every season. Help me trust Your timing for fruitfulness and keep my faith unwavering, even when I don't see immediate results. Thank You for being my source of life and nourishment. In Jesus' name. Amen.

Day 27

He Is So Faithful

SCRIPTURE

"I will bless the Lord at all times; His praise shall continually be in my mouth." — Psalm 34:1 (NKJV)

DEVOTIONAL

One morning, I woke up with Psalm 34:1 on my heart. As I read the entire chapter, I couldn't help but reflect on how faithful God had been that week. We had been praying for Patrick, my husband, to get a job, and God answered. Then, as we tried to navigate the schedule conflicts that came with it, I prayed for free help with my daughter, Sahra, and He provided that, too!

So often, we pray and move on without pausing to recognize how God has truly come through for us. But today, I am reminded that His goodness is always present. Even in the transitions and unknowns, He is working things out before we even know to ask. My heart is full of gratitude because God's provision has once again proven that He cares about the details of our lives.

Psalm 34 is not just a call to praise when things are going well; it is an invitation to trust and bless the Lord at all times. Even when things seem uncertain or

challenging, our response should be praise. Not because life is always smooth, but because God is always faithful.

SONG

— *"Great Is Thy Faithfulness"(Choose any version of the rendition or sing straight from a hymnal).*

GRATITUDE

Write three things you are grateful for today. For me, I am so grateful to my friends who helped us when we needed help with Sahra while we navigated our clashing schedules.

PRAYER

Father, I bless Your name today because You are faithful in every season. Thank You for answered prayers, for provision, and for always working things out for our good. Help me to continually praise You, not just when things go well, but in every circumstance. Let my heart remain steadfast in gratitude, knowing You are always near. In Jesus' name. Amen.

Day 28

Already Approved

"I knew you before I formed you in your mother's womb. Before you were born I set you apart and appointed you as my prophet to the nations." - Jeremiah 1:5 (NLT)

DEVOTIONAL

For much of my life, I believed love had to be earned. I thought being good, helpful, and impressive was the way to be noticed. I carried that same belief into my relationship with God. I assumed that if I prayed more, did more, gave more, or served more, then maybe *just maybe*, God would be more proud of me. Just maybe this would be my breakthrough or my blessing because I have been so good. *Wait, is this Santa's Naughty or Nice list?*

As the song "Jireh" by Maverick City Music expresses, I don't hold God up, and *"there's nothing I can do to let You down."* It quietly broke the lie I was entertaining.

It hit me: God is not depending on me to keep Him pleased. His love does not move up or down based on my behavior. He is steady. Faithful. Unchanging. I am **fully loved**, even when I feel unworthy or unseen.

Think about that: *You are not earning God's attention. You already have it.*

You are not trying to become worthy. You were created worthy because *He said so.*

When God told Jeremiah, *"Before I formed you in the womb, I knew you,"* He was not just speaking to a prophet. He was revealing His heart for all of us. He is not waiting for us to become someone great; He already sees greatness in who He created.

This does not mean we do not grow or change. But the change is no longer rooted in fear of rejection; it is rooted in the safety of being accepted. We do not perform to belong; we live freely *because* we belong. That kind of love brings rest to the soul. It silences shame. It softens the heart. You do not have to do anything special today to be worthy of God's love. You are already loved. You are already approved.

SONG

— *"Jireh" by Maverick City*

GRATITUDE

Write three things you are grateful for. Today, I am grateful that this workweek has been steady and that I was able to work at my own pace. In the nursing world, this is huge in the hospital setting.

PRAYER

Father, thank You for knowing me fully and loving me completely. Forgive me for striving to prove my worth when You have already declared it. Remind me that I

do not need to earn what You have already freely given. Teach me to rest in Your approval and to walk confidently in the identity You gave me. Let Your voice be louder than the world's. In Jesus' name. Amen.

Day 29

Sow Anyway—Living Boldly From a Secure Heart

SCRIPTURE

"Plant your seed in the morning and keep busy all afternoon, for you don't know if profit will come from one activity or another—or maybe both." - Ecclesiastes 11:6 (NLT)

DEVOTIONAL

This is an invitation to keep sowing.

You have made it through 28 days of pulling up the weeds of performance, perfectionism, and pressure, and now you are rooted, grounded in truth, anchored in grace, and secure in love.

But do not stop here.

Ecclesiastes 11 is not about overthinking outcomes; it is about trusting God enough to live boldly and take the next step, even if you do not know where it will lead or if you cannot predict the harvest. When your identity is no longer tied to the results, you are free to walk in obedience, not fear.

You do not need to be certain. You just need to be secure in Him.

This final day is not about finishing strong for the sake of appearances. It is about beginning again with the confidence that your security is not based on what you do, but on who He is.

So, go ahead and love big. Speak up. Try the new thing. Rest when He says rest. Work when He says move. Share your story. Be faithful with what is in your hands because your roots go deep now, and your life—your everyday life—is a seed in His hands.

SONG

— *"Firm Foundation (He Won't)" by Maverick City Music*

Let this song anchor you in the truth that though the winds may blow, your foundation will not shake. He is faithful. He will not fail.

GRATITUDE

Write three things you are grateful for. Today, I am grateful that I get the opportunity to help nursing students in the clinical setting. I enjoy teaching and sharing my knowledge, and it is nice to know that it is needed and appreciated.

PRAYER

Lord, thank You for taking me on this journey, from striving to security, from performance to peace. I no longer need all the answers to move forward. I trust You with the process, and I trust You with the outcome.

Give me boldness to plant good seeds today and wisdom to leave the harvest in Your hands. Thank You that I do not sow alone, You are with me in every season. In Jesus' name. Amen.

A Place to Linger in Worship

Some days, you will have the words to pray. Other days, worship will carry you when your words feel heavy or hard to find.

This devotional was never meant to end when the pages do. It was meant to lead you into a rhythm of presence, trust, and rest that continues beyond these pages. These songs are not assignments. They are invitations. You do not need to listen to all of them, and you do not need to listen in any particular order. Simply choose what meets you where you are.

Let this be a place you return to when you need stillness, when you are waiting, or when praise feels like the only response your heart can offer.

For Stillness, Awe, and Abiding

- **Such an Awesome God** – Maverick City Music
- **Defender** – Francesca Battistelli
- **You Still Love Me** – Tasha Cobbs Leonard
- **Forever at your feet**- Tasha Cobbs Leonard

For Trusting God in the Waiting and the Fight

- **Never Lost** – CeCe Winans
- **Hard Fought Hallelujah** – Brandon Lake
- **Worship Rise** – Travis Greene

For Praise, Strength, and Confident Faith

- **Praise You Anywhere** – Brandon Lake
- **Get Ready for Overflow** – Tasha Cobbs Leonard
- **Praise** – Elevation Worship
- **Worthy** – Elevation Worship
- **Living Room Session** – Elevation Worship
- **Mighty Name of Jesus** – The Belonging Co
- **Worthy** – Indiana Bible College

May these songs help you remain rooted, anchored, and secure.

May worship continue to quiet striving, strengthen faith, and remind your heart that God is near, faithful, and worthy in every season.

About the Author

Samantha McCormack is a nurse, wife, mother, and aspiring writer who is passionate about helping women find grace in the everyday. With a heart for faith and simplicity, she writes devotionals and encouragement rooted in scripture and real life. Samantha lives in Florida with her husband, Patrick, their daughter, Sahra, and her mom, Eveling, where she is learning (daily) to trade pressure for presence, and to walk freely in the love of Jesus.

www.ingramcontent.com/pod-product-compliance
Lightning Source LLC
LaVergne TN
LVHW010937110826
845149LV00013B/2637

* 9 7 8 1 9 6 6 7 2 3 3 8 7 *